VICTORIA & ALFRED

Waterfront

CAPE TOWN, SOUTH AFRICA

VICTORIA & ALFRED

CAPE TOWN, SOUTH AFRICA

Living, working, shopping, playing, wining and dining in an atmosphere of scenic splendour and sophistication in a historic working harbour – Cape Town's unique V&A Waterfront is renowned the world over.

GERALD HOBERMAN

In association with

THE GERALD & MARC HOBERMAN COLLECTION
CAPE TOWN · LONDON · NEW YORK

CONTENTS

Photography, text, design and production control: Gerald Hoberman
Reproduction: Marc Hoberman
Design and layout: Christian Jaggers
Editing and additional text: Roelien Theron
Index: Ethleen Lastovica

www.hobermancollection.com

ISBN 1-919939-28-8   ISBN 978-1-919939-28-5

Victoria & Alfred Waterfront is published by The Gerald & Marc Hoberman Collection (Pty) Ltd
Reg. No. 99/00167/07. PO Box 60044, Victoria Junction, 8005, Cape Town, South Africa
Telephone: 27-21-419 6657/419 2210 Fax: 27-21-418 5987 e-mail: office@hobermancollection.com

in association with the V&A Waterfront (Pty) Ltd
Telephone: 27-21-408 7600 Fax: 27-21-408 7605 e-mail: info@waterfront.co.za
www.waterfront.co.za

International marketing, corporate sales and picture library

United Kingdom, Republic of Ireland, Europe
Marc Hoberman
Hoberman Collection (UK)
250 Kings Road, London, SW3 5UE
Telephone: 0207 352 1315 Fax: 0207 352 4617
e-mail: uk@hobermancollection.com

United States of America, Canada, Asia
Laurence R. Bard
Hoberman Collection (USA), Inc. / Una Press, Inc.
PO Box 880206, Boca Raton, FL 33488, USA
Telephone: (561) 542 1141
e-mail: hobcolus@bellsouth.net

For copies of this book printed with your company's logo and corporate message contact The Gerald & Marc Hoberman Collection.
For international requests contact Hoberman Collection (UK).

Other titles in this series by The Gerald & Marc Hoberman Collection

ENGLISH				**GERMAN**	**FRENCH**	**SPANISH**	**JAPANESE**
Cape Town	Ireland	San Francisco	Wildlife	Afrikas Wildnis	L'Afrique du Sud	Ciudad del Cabo	London
England	KwaZulu-Natal	South Africa	Wildlife of Africa	Die Tierwelt	La Faune Africaine	Fauna Africana	**ITALIAN**
Franschhoek &	London	South Africa's		Kapstadt	Le Cap	Sudáfrica	Namibia
Rickety Bridge	Namibia	Winelands		London	Londres		
D'vine Restaurant	Napa Valley	of the Cape		Namibia	Namibie		
– The Cookbook	New York	Teddy Bears		Südafrika			
	Salt Lake City	Washington, D.C.					

Agents and distributors

Germany	*Namibia*	*Republic of Ireland and Northern Ireland*	*United Kingdom*	*United States of America, Canada and Asia*
Herold Verlagsauslieferung & Logistik GmbH	Projects & Promotions cc	GSR Distributors Ltd	DJ Segrue Ltd	Hoberman Collection (USA), Inc. / Una Press, Inc.
Raiffeisenallee 10	PO Box 96102	47 Marley Court	7c Bourne Road	PO Box 880206
82041 Oberhaching	Windhoek	Dublin 14	Bushey, Hertfordshire	Boca Raton, FL 33488
Tel: (089) 61 38 710	Tel: (0)61-25 5715/6	Tel: (0)1-295 1205	WD23 3NH	Tel: (561) 542 1141
Fax: (089) 61 38 7120	Fax: (0)61-23 0033	Fax: (0)1-296 6403	Tel: (0)7976-273 225	e-mail: hobcolus@bellsouth.net
e-mail: herold@herold-va.de	e-mail: proprom@iafrica.com.na	e-mail: murray47@eircom.net	Fax: (0)20-8421 9577	
			e-mail: sales@djsegrue.co.uk	

Printed in Singapore

ACKNOWLEDGEMENTS

I am most appreciative to have been entrusted with such an important book by the management and staff of the V&A Waterfront. It has been a delight to have been so well received by the tenants and the many other people I have interacted with in photographing and writing about the wonderful Waterfront.

Inspiration and alacrity blossomed into unbridled energy and enthusiasm as the project got under way and the book began to evolve. This was in no small measure due to the sterling support of the V&A Waterfront community of hoteliers, restaurant owners, brewers, shop owners, crafters, entertainers, leisure boat operators, dock workers and the many visitors from near and far.

To my staff at The Hoberman Collection in Cape Town and London, especially Magda Bosch, Justin Buchanan, Tarryn Clarke-McLeod, Colin Friend, Kevin Gie, Christian Jaggers and Gavin Smith, my son Marc and my editor Roelien Theron, thank you for your support and expertise.

I would also like to thank the many people who went out of their way to assist me on this project, especially the following:

Tina Alics	Russell Furlong	Russell Matchette	Yair Shimansky
Chris Barnard	Shelley Garb	Andrew Mphanga	Ralph Shulman
Steven Bentley	Craig Girdlestone	Salifou Mbombo	Leavelle Snow
Lauraine Bester	Aldo Girolo	Nicole McCreedy	Trudy Southgate
Natasha Bester	Linda Girolo	Ike Mndini	Anina Stapelberg
Henriette Boschoff	Jack Goldblatt	Sabelo Mkwetyana	Francois Steyn
Saskia Brown	Colin Goodman	Janet Moss	'The Victoria Four' (Peter
Doris Bruwer	Olga Goodman	Thinus Mostert	Abrahams, Davie Fields,
Patience Cabuko	Donald Greig	Washington Mtimkulu	William Jales, S. Petersen)
Matthew Cannon	Jillian Grindley-Ferris	Jeremy Nel	Marie-Louise Trautman
Patrick Chauke	Peet Grobbelaar	Linda Ntshinga	Ann Tripp
William Coates	Hayley Herlitz	Nicholas Paul	Sue van Diggele
Mirriam Dlamini	Simphiwe Hoboshe	Ross Phinn	Peter Johan Veldsman
Selina Dube	Rui Jardim	Julie-Ann Plaatjies	Rejeanne Viletman
Hanri Du Toit	Vaughan Johnson	Garry Raa	Marc Wright
Arie Fabian	Ajit Kanakia	Anthony Roodt	
Jason Fischer	Helen S. Lockhart	Shadleigh Roscoe	

VICTORIA & ALFRED
Waterfront

CAPE TOWN, SOUTH AFRICA

CAPE TOWN

Robben Island
5.75 sea miles / 11.4 km

VICTORIA BASIN

ALFRED
BASIN

V&A
WATERFRONT
MARINA

N

1 Two Oceans Aquarium
2 Breakwater parking garage
   development
3 Chavonnes Battery
4 Clock Tower
5 Clock Tower Centre
6 Waterfront Craft Market
   & Wellness Centre
7 Cape Town International
   Convention Centre
8 East Pier
9 Fish Quay
10 Robinson Graving Dock
11 Jetty One
12 Jetty Two
13 Market Square & Amphitheatre
14 Marina residential and
   hotel development
15 Nobel Square
16 Old Port Captain's Office
17 Pierhead & Swing-bridge
18 Quay 4
19 Quay 5
20 Quay 6
21 Quay 7
22 Red Shed Craft Workshop
23 Robben Island Museum and ferries
24 South Arm
25 T Jetty
26 UCT Graduate School of Business
27 Alfred Mall
28 Victoria Wharf Shopping Centre

INTRODUCTION

At the southernmost tip of the vast African continent is a waterfront of unrivalled scenic splendour. Set in a working harbour in Cape Town, the V&A Waterfront attracts vast numbers of locals and visitors from far and wide. Visible from the water's edge towards the City Bowl is spectacular Table Mountain and its famous cableway. It is flanked by Devil's Peak to the left, Lion's Head and Signal Hill to the right, and, along the Atlantic Seaboard, the Twelve Apostles. Just beyond Table Bay lies Robben Island, where former South African President Nelson Mandela was once incarcerated.

The V&A Waterfront is privately owned and is very well managed. It is diverse, vibey, user friendly and accessible. It can be reached by car, shuttle bus, taxi, water taxi, boat and even helicopter. Secure free parking and paid underground parking garages are available.

The V&A Waterfront – affectionately referred to as 'the V&A' or 'the Waterfront' – is most conveniently situated. If you intend staying in one of its superb hotels, you will be within easy reach of access roads to the famous Kirstenbosch National Botanical Garden, the delightful African penguin colony at Boulders beach, the dramatic promontory at the tip of the Cape Peninsula, known as Cape Point, and the spectacular winelands of the Cape. Just a short ride away are the world-famous Table Mountain National Park and the ever popular Clifton and Camps Bay beaches.

If, however, you choose to spend your time at the Waterfront, you will rub shoulders with a diverse crowd of South Africans and visitors from around the world. It is a shopper's paradise, with every whim,

fancy and speciality catered for. High-fashion boutiques stock international designer brands alongside sought-after local brands. The Waterfront is also a great place to buy good art and artefacts from elsewhere in Africa.

The V&A is where you can dine on anything that takes your fancy: a humble hot dog and a cool drink or a lavish seafood spread accompanied by an excellent local wine in an award-winning restaurant with spectacular harbour-side views.

For those wanting to eat ethnic food, the options are endless: African, Cape Malay, Portuguese, Indian, Japanese, Chinese, Greek, Mexican, American, English, Middle Eastern, Italian, German, Belgian, Fusion and more.

Love beer? There are three different breweries all offering superb beers. Prefer whiskey and a Cuban cigar? There is an incredible variety at Bascule Bar in the elegant Cape Grace Hotel, one of several hotels at the Waterfront, with more under construction.

Street entertainers are everywhere – from male choirs and marimba bands to mime artists and buskers. For added entertainment, various festivals and events are held throughout the year.

Several large corporations and businesses now operate from the Waterfront. There are banks, financial institutions, bookshops, wine shops, health spas, jewellers and diamond cutters. Added to the buzz is the constant arrival of passenger ships, luxury liners and cargo ships. The Waterfront is characterised by a seamless integration of fishing, commercial and industrial businesses as well as tourism and entertainment venues, all in the context of a working harbour. It is no wonder that this award-winning enterprise continues to be a success story with an impressive year-on-year growth rate in terms of both development and popularity.

The intrepid Portuguese explorer, Bartolomeu Dias rounded the Cape in 1488. He named it Cabo das Tormentas – *Cape of Storms*. King John II of Portugal later renamed it Cabo da Boa Esperança – *the Cape of Good Hope*. Sir Francis Drake, who passed the Cape on 18 June 1580, presumably in finer weather conditions than did Dias, declared it to be 'the most stately thing and the fairest cape we saw in the whole circumference of the earth'.

But no settlement was established until the Dutch East India Company set up a refreshment station at the Cape in April 1652 to supply its ships en route to the East with fresh vegetables, meat and water – vital necessities to combat the scourge of scurvy. This was the historical origin of what ultimately was to evolve into the V&A Waterfront in 1998, some 346 years later.

Table Bay, despite its majestic setting, was never a natural harbour. Its gently curving bay is vulnerable to north-westerly gales, tempestuous storms and dense fogs in winter. The first safe moorings – the Victoria and Alfred basins – were built during Victorian times. They were augmented by the larger docks and contemporary container facilities in use today.

My earliest personal association with Cape Town harbour was as a young boy accompanying my late father, Michael Hoberman, who would go there to organise the logistics of bunkering coal or anthracite on ships for our family business. He was a popular figure at the docks, having arranged to coal warships in the dead of night throughout the Second World War. I remember his many stories of his experiences at the harbour. He would recount tales of when his grandfather imported coal from the Hamilton L. Colliery in Wales, which arrived at the Cape Town harbour in sailing ships. The quality-conscious Hobermans paid an extra shilling per tonne to stow the coal 'tween decks instead of in the hold, to minimise pulverisation of the coal as the ship listed on the high seas. This was in the days before coal was mined in the then Transvaal and transported by rail to the Cape.

I recall the vibrant Harbour Café, then a wood-and-iron building that was open seven days a week. Ready-cooked crayfish was sold at the harbour gates for two shillings and sixpence each. A huge bag of crayfish legs was a mere nine pence!

This historic spirit of the harbour and of 'old Cape Town' was revived with the development of the V&A Waterfront. It has been a great privilege for me and The Hoberman Collection to take the photographs and produce the text for this book. The book is not encyclopaedic, nor does it attempt to be all encompassing, for such a publication would make an excellent doorstop in a Southeaster. It would also be far too expensive and impractical for visitors and tourists to take home. This book, it is hoped, captures the spirit, essence and romance of the extraordinary V&A Waterfront, making it a perfect memento and an enticement to return with friends who have never visited the city.

Gerald Hoberman

GERALD HOBERMAN
V&A Waterfront, Cape Town

V&A WATERFRONT

Nestled between sea and mountain, the V&A Waterfront is one of South Africa's premier tourist attractions. Billed as *the* place to 'live, work, shop and play', the Waterfront – a combination of a working harbour and leisure, shopping, residential and office facilities with unrivalled scenic splendour – is one of the most successful dockland renewal projects in the world. Its array of shopping centres, luxury hotels, conference facilities, craft markets, cinemas, music and entertainment venues, restaurants and coffee shops attracts locals and tourists alike. The Waterfront's three shopping centres, the Victoria Wharf, the Clock Tower Centre and the Alfred Mall are major draw-cards. The double-level Victoria Wharf

12

(above and opposite right) was the first to open its doors, in the early 1990s. Its architecture was inspired by the original Victorian-style warehouses, coal sheds and residences of the historic harbour. The spacious interior is distinctly modern, with contemporary finishes, high ceilings, large skylights and wide walkways – all of which make shopping at its many department and retail stores, speciality and curio shops a most pleasant experience. The shops in the renovated Clock Tower (opposite top left) and the Alfred Mall (opposite bottom left) complement the many shopping attractions of Victoria Wharf. Both centres boast numerous restaurants, coffee shops, pubs and taverns, as well as a wide range of boutiques and speciality, art and curio shops.

NEVER A DULL MOMENT

The V&A Waterfront is a hive of activity with year-round events, exhibitions, entertainment and sporting challenges catering for a wide range of tastes and different age groups, from the very young to the very old. Music lovers can listen to the lively sounds of some highly accomplished buskers or enjoy live performances at the Amphitheatre (opposite), near the Victoria Wharf Shopping Centre. It is here that the annual Jazzathon is held, showcasing some of Cape Town's finest talent. From the Amphitheatre, it is a short walk to the Nelson Mandela Gateway, from where high-speed catamarans take visitors to Robben Island for a two-and-a-half hour tour that includes a visit to Nelson Mandela's prison

cell. Visitors to the Waterfront can also undertake one of four self-guided walking routes, visit a working brewery, enjoy boat trips, charter a helicopter, stroll through the Two Oceans Aquarium, see a movie, admire the harbour's historic buildings and heritage sites or visit the Iziko South African Maritime Museum. Other activities include those of the National Sea Rescue Institute, which has one of its thirty rescue bases at the V&A Waterfront (opposite left). But if what is required is a relaxed afternoon in the sun, there are watering holes and coffee shops aplenty from which to watch the crowds and enjoy the spectacular views.

TWO OCEANS AQUARIUM

The Two Oceans Aquarium at the V&A Waterfront is home to some 3 000 sea creatures, most of which come from the two oceans that meet at the southern tip of Africa – the Indian and the Atlantic. The Kelp Forest Exhibit is a popular exhibit and one of only two such displays in the world, the other being at Monterey Bay Aquarium in the United States of America. The 800 000-litre Kelp Forest Exhibit showcases the giant kelp forests that dominate the rocky shores off South Africa's west coast and the cold-water fish that populate them. This forest remains one of the aquarium's biggest draw-cards, and many visitors return time and time again to enjoy its beauty and tranquillity.

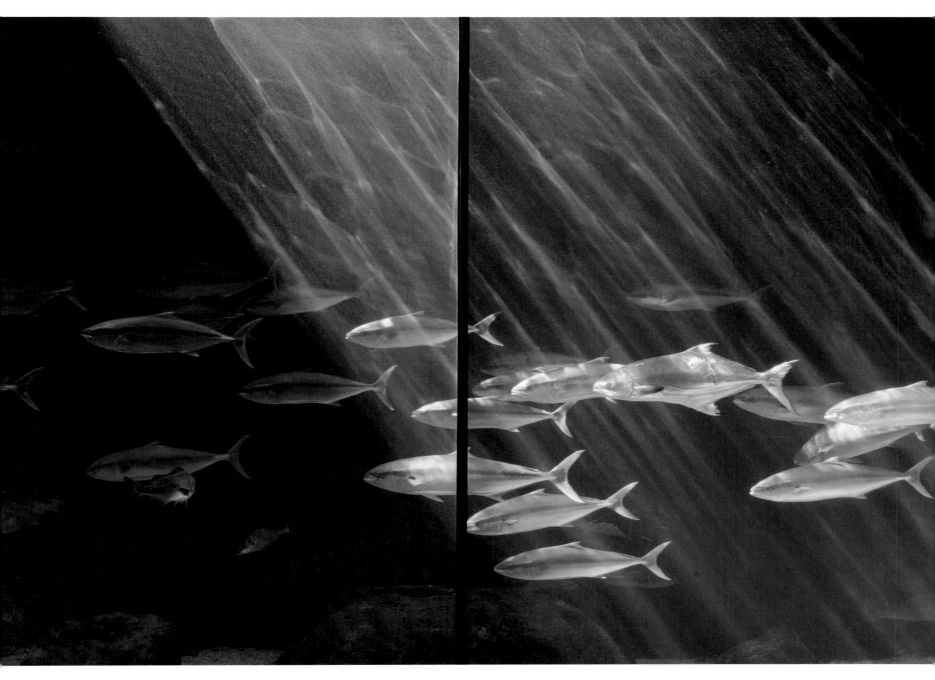

I&J PREDATOR EXHIBIT

Containing two million litres of seawater, the enormous 11-metre wide and 4-metre high I&J Predator Exhibit at the Two Oceans Aquarium provides a dramatic window on piscine life along South Africa's coast. Large ragged-tooth sharks patrol the waters of this exhibit while an assortment of predatory fish, graceful rays and a loggerhead turtle appear to swim effortlessly against the 1-knot current in the tank. Members of the public who desire a closer encounter with the aquarium's predators can sign up for a shark dive – as long they have a scuba-diving qualification.

OCEAN DWELLERS

While most sea creatures avoid anemones because of the stinging cells in their tentacles, Western clownfish (*Amphiprion ocellaris*) (top left) live closely with anemones in a symbiotic partnership, which can last a lifetime. Giant spider crabs (*Macrocheira kaempferi*) (top right) are the largest crustaceans in the world: males grow to approximately 1 metre in height with a 4-metre leg stretch. Juvenile semicircle angelfish (*Pomacanthus semicirculatus*) (bottom left) differ in colouration from adult angelfish, so much so that they look like a different species. Juveniles are navy blue to black with alternating blue and white bars in a semicircle. Adult angelfish have greenish bodies with blue flecks. The giant moray eel

(*Gymnothorax javanicus*) (opposite bottom right) is a graceful animal but its sheer size of 1.5 metres in length and 50 centimetres in girth is enough to instil just a tad of fear in onlookers. Giant moray eels can reach lengths of up to 3 metres and weigh as much as 25 kilograms. Clown triggerfish (*Balistoides conspicillum*) (above) are so named because of the prominent trigger-like first dorsal spine which can be locked into an upright position by the second dorsal spine. Triggerfish use this spine to defend themselves and also to lodge themselves into crevices on a reef when threatened by potential predators. The family name *Balistoides* is derived from the Latin word *ballista*, which refers to the Roman catapult. The name thus alludes to the catapult-like device of the dorsal spines.

WATERFRONT VILLAGE

Overlooking the V&A Waterfront Marina, Waterfront Village offers holiday makers, travellers and business delegates a luxurious home away from home. The collection of self-catering and serviced apartments, managed by Village & Life, combines all the comforts of a first-class hotel with the spontaneity and freedom of home.

More than eighty stylishly furnished apartments and penthouses, with one, two or three bedrooms, are on offer. The apartments vary in size from 65 m² to 300 m². Stays can range from one night to several months.

A full concierge service is available to take care of visitors' every whim and fancy. The service includes making restaurant bookings, arranging sight-seeing tours and helicopter trips and even chartering boats.

Discerning visitors and high-profile celebrities wishing to entertain or have business meetings in the privacy of their apartments can order their very own butler, executive chef and waiters for the occasion.

The Waterfront Village is conveniently situated close to top-flight restaurants, bars and other amenities

OLD PORT CAPTAIN'S OFFICE

Visible from Quay 5 across a section of the Victoria Basin, the old Port Captain's Office building (lit up in the distance) is an iconic feature of the V&A Waterfront. This beautifully restored, blue-and-white gabled landmark building was erected in 1904 during a period of rapid expansion of the Cape Town harbour. At the time it replaced the smaller port captain's office in the historic Clock Tower building on the other side of the entrance to the Alfred Basin. The new building was used as a lookout by shipping controllers and berthing staff.

CRUISING FOR PLEASURE

The discovery in South Africa of diamonds in 1867 and gold in 1886 led to a huge influx of people from all over the world. The evolution of bigger and better steamships coupled with an improvement in the facilities at the Cape Town harbour brought even more people to the growing city. Towards the end of the nineteenth century, many shipping lines, including the Union, dropped anchor at Cape Town. Some provided a spirited sea voyage that included lavish dining, deck games, libraries, live entertainment and dancing. Today this tradition lives on in cruise ships such as the *Europa*, one of the most luxurious of its kind to berth at the Waterfront.

25

AFRICAN TRADING PORT

Business is brisk at the African Trading Port, a fascinating curio shop located in the historic Port Captain's Office building at the V&A Waterfront. It is full to capacity with artworks and artefacts collected from across Africa. The shop has one of the biggest Shona sculpture collections in the world and a large collection of West African art. It also stocks gold and silver jewellery and ceramic objects. One of the most admired pieces is this Bamileke statue (above) from Cameroon. The Bamileke are a collection of different groups that have settled in the grasslands of western Cameroon. Each group has its own king, or *fon*, and most Bamileke statues represent the *fon*. The Kuba belt decorated with cowry shells and

African beads (above left) originates from the Democratic Republic of the Congo. Traditionally, two similar belts are worn across the chest. The Kuba live in a region of valleys in central DRC. The brightly painted Tuareg leather cloth (top right) is richly embellished with plastic stripes and mirrors. Tuareg cloths are made from goat and camel hides and are used, for example, as bags and wall hangings. Tuareg societies can be found across the Sahara from Algeria to Niger. Vibrant colours and designs characterise the dress cloth (bottom right) used by both men and women in many African countries.

ART FROM AFRICA

Whether a serious collector or an impulsive buyer, you are destined to find something fascinating at the African Trading Port. Objects to choose from include: from Nigeria, wooden boards painted in oils to advertise barber shops (bottom left); from the Ivory Coast, colonial figures handcarved out of wood and decorated with oil paint (bottom centre and right); and, from Nigeria, a Yoruba beaded statue of a woman holding a chicken, traditionally placed in a king's residence (top left). To the right of this image is a series of details of a door-frame from Cameroon. These are used at the entrance of a village elder's or a chief's residence or a granary.

CARROL BOYES FUNCTIONAL ART

The Carrol Boyes flagship store at the V&A Waterfront has proved to be a phenomenal success. Widely regarded as one of South Africa's most influential designers, Carrol Boyes is world-famous for her distinctive range of designer homeware created from pewter, aluminium and stainless steel. A former teacher, she left the profession in the late 1980s to establish Carrol Boyes Functional Art. Since then, the company has created more than 2 000 contemporary products for use in the kitchen and home. New products are designed at the Cape Town head office and manufactured in the Limpopo province. They are then transported to Cape Town for a quality check before being shipped to outlets in forty countries worldwide.

THE GREEN DOLPHIN RESTAURANT

This seaside venue, in its own words, is 'dedicated to the preservation of jazz eight nights a week'. Since opening its doors in 1990, the Green Dolphin Restaurant – named after Louis Armstrong's earliest recording – has provided live jazz, good food and fine wine 365 days of the year. While the menu, wine list and fresh sea breeze are incentive enough to visit the Green Dolphin, it is really the music – presented in three sets beginning just after eight and ending around midnight – that draws the crowds. Its list of featured artists reads like a 'Who's Who' in the world of South African and international jazz. Superstar Natalie Cole has been known to pop in. Jonathan Butler, Hugh Masekela, Herb Ellis, Darius

Brubeck, Gavin Minter, Robbie Jansen, Errol Dyers, Duke and Ezra Ngcukana and Earl Okin have all performed there. So have divas Sylvia Mdunyelwa, Tina Schouw, Judith Sephuma and Australian singer/songwriter Missy Higgins. Patrons know there is never a dull moment at the Waterfront's oldest jazz venue. So too do countless embassies in South Africa, which regularly request the Green Dolphin to host jazz musicians from their respective countries. With an uninterrupted record of almost 6 000 consecutive nights of live jazz to date, the Green Dolphin Restaurant has more than lived up to its original pledge of being dedicated to the preservation of jazz.

EMILY'S RESTAURANT

Owner of Emily's Restaurant, renowned food author and famous media personality, Peter Veldsman (centre) is an award-winning connoisseur of fine dining. He has an impish twinkle in his eyes that suggests an underlying sense of humour, which he skillfully combines with an impeccable sense of occasion. All this makes for dramatic dining in one of the most stylish spaces in the luxury Clock Tower at the V&A Waterfront.

The menu is distinctly South African, mixed with some European influences, and only the finest ingredients from all over the African continent are used. On the home front, Veldsman and chef Johan Odendaal are responsible for creating signature dishes that have put South African cuisine on the international map. Infused with what the pair call 'Zulu-zest, Sotho-exotica, Tswana-touches, Xhosa-putu and mysterious Malay', the approach to local dishes makes for a distinctly original menu that reveals the true flavours of the country. Odendaal is assisted in the kitchen by head chef Andrew Whelan (right) and trainee chef Louis Badenhorst (left).

The fact that foodies around the world have taken note of Emily's is evident in the long list of awards this accomplished eatery has garnered since its humble beginnings as an informal bistro in Cape Town: Diners Club International Platinum and rare Diamond awards, BBC award winner, *The New York Times* accolade recipient, New Millennium Award by the Tourist, Hotel and Catering Industry, Golden Europe Award for Quality, Wine Magazine awards, various Top 10 awards, and the Tony Jackman Choice award.

OLGA JEWELLERY DESIGN STUDIO

One of South Africa's leading jewellery makers, Olga Goodman designs unique jewellery for discerning clients to their specific tastes. These designs are then transformed into exquisite masterpieces handcrafted by a team of master goldsmiths and diamond cutters at the Olga Jewellery Design Studio in the Victoria Wharf Shopping Centre at the V&A Waterfront. Diamonds and tanzanite are central to her collection, and are combined with gold, silver and platinum. Believing that women should be able to wear their jewellery with style and confidence – whether it be with a ball gown, a designer outfit or comfortable day wear – Goodman creates jewellery pieces that reflect a passionate love for design

and a philosophy of versatility, freshness and sensuality. In her quest for perfection, Goodman is assisted by her husband, Colin, a leading jewellery manufacturer who plays an important role in ensuring the smooth running of her highly successful enterprise. The duo travel internationally and regularly attend jewellery fairs to keep abreast with the latest trends in design and manufacturing. The ideas and stimulation gained from these experiences are used to further develop the Olga collection. Glamorous jewellery that would make enduring mementos of the Waterfront experience include a variety of diamond rings (opposite), tanzanite and diamonds set in necklaces and rings (top and bottom left) and a beautiful solitaire diamond ring (right).

UCT GRADUATE SCHOOL OF BUSINESS AND BREAKWATER LODGE

The old Industrial Breakwater Prison on Portswood Road in the V&A Waterfront was built in 1901. It was an addition to the original Breakwater Prison built in 1860 on Portswood Ridge to house convicts working on the construction of Cape Town's first breakwater and harbour. The design of the prison included an enclosed courtyard and four castellated turrets and was based on that of Millbank and Pentonville prisons in England. Today this building houses one of the top business schools in South Africa, the University of Cape Town Graduate School of Business, as well as the Breakwater Lodge, the Waterfront's leading budget hotel operated by Protea Hotels.

TREADMILL, OLD BREAKWATER PRISON

This relic of the Victorian penal system is a grim reminder of the harsh, inhumane punishments meted out to prisoners at the original Breakwater Prison, often for trivial misdemeanours. Built in 1890, the treadmill (top right) was one of the worst forms of punishment used at the prison: it was like ascending an endless flight of stairs for no other purpose than to penalise the prisoner. If a prisoner could not keep up the pace, his shins would be lacerated by the steps of the revolving wheel. The restored treadmill can be seen at the end of a row of former isolation cells in the upper parking area of the Breakwater Lodge.

MEMORIES ETCHED IN STONE

Not much is known about the individuals who carved this graffiti on the stone walls of the Breakwater Prison. Segments of the preserved prison wall show a warrior, the Union Jack and an early version of the Australian coat of arms. Another commemorates the relief of Mafeking during the South African War (1899–1902). These bear testimony to the many Breakwater prisoners held here between 1860 and 1926. Not all of the prisoners were convicted criminals; some were prisoners of war. Among the more famous of the Breakwater prisoners was a group of San or Bushmen whose descriptions of their beliefs, traditions and culture were recorded by the German linguist W.H.I. Bleek and his sister-in-law Lucy Lloyd.

CHAVONNES BATTERY

The Chavonnes Battery (top row, bottom left) is one of the oldest European structures in South Africa. Built between 1714 and 1725, it was one of several defensive positions erected along the Cape shoreline to protect the Dutch settlement against trade rivals from Europe. The battery was later used to confine crew members and passengers with contagious illnesses, including smallpox, until they were declared fit. The battery was decommissioned in 1861. The battery is on Clock Tower Square, and is open to the public for viewing. Also at the V&A Waterfront is a replica of a sculpture created by Swedish artist Carl Frederick Reuterswärd in 1980 in support of non-violence (bottom right).

THE COMMODORE

Located in the V&A Waterfront, the luxurious five-star Commodore is one of Cape Town's most elegant hotels. As its name suggests, a strong nautical theme is evident in the stylish design of its interiors. Authentic brass portholes are featured at the entrance to the reception area – a warm and inviting space decorated with old maps, pictures of sailing boats, ships in glass boxes, a brass cannon and various nautical instruments. Beyond the reception area, the lounge's comfortable leather couches and a large fireplace make it a rather agreeable place for a quiet read or an elegant repose after a meal in the hotel's Clipper Restaurant. Guests can relax in the s.k.i.n. Commodore wellness spa, conveniently situated in the hotel.

THE PORTSWOOD

The four-star Portswood is a haven of tranquillity for leisure and business travellers. All the facilities one might expect from a luxury hotel are here: elegant bedrooms, business services, a swimming pool, same-day laundry and a chauffeur service. Thoroughly modern, the building also includes historical relics discovered during its construction. One such feature is an old well that was used to supply water in the Portswood Ridge area. The restored well can be viewed in the hotel's reception area (bottom left). The historical theme is repeated in the hotel's Quarterdeck Restaurant (top right), which is housed in a section of the former old Breakwater Prison where convicts who worked on the harbour's first breakwater were held.

THE CLOCK TOWER

This magnificent Victorian-era octagonal clock tower painted a colour similar to that of its original brickwork is situated on Clock Tower Square. An icon of the old Cape Town docks and a symbol of the V&A Waterfront, it stands sentinel over the comings and goings of the busy harbour – just as it has ever since its completion in 1882 as the first port captain's office. Since then it has served duty as a reading room for visiting ship captains and as an office building for fishing giant, Irvin & Johnson. The building was restored in 1997. The mechanism of its elegant clock was made in Edinburgh, Scotland, by J.A. Richie & Son in 1883. The clock was restored in 1976. On the ground floor of the tower is a tide gauge which, when

operational, allowed passing vessels to determine the ebb and flow of the harbour waters. The wall of the stairwell leading to the second floor is graced by a painting of the Madonna and child. The second floor features a mirror room, which gave the port captain 'eyes at the back of his head', thus enabling him to have a view of all activities in the docks. Today this room houses a restaurant serving light meals, which is run by famous restaurateur Peter Veldsman of the nearby Emily's Restaurant. An elegant swing-bridge links the Clock Tower Precinct with the Pierhead.

MITCHELL'S WATERFRONT BREWERY

Lex Mitchell opened the first Mitchell's Brewery in Knysna in the southern Cape in 1983. Six years later the company established Mitchell's Waterfront Brewery, the first brewery to become part of the revitalised V&A Waterfront. The brewery has since changed hands, and new owner Atholl Mitchell has kept up the tradition of producing complex beers with flavours that mellow in the mouth. Favourites such as Forester's Draught, Bosun's Bitter, Raven Stout and Old Wobbly are all brewed on location to the finest standards. So are the evocatively named 90 Shilling Ale, a spicy beer that has a gloriously round, full palate and Milk & Honey, which has a glow as golden as the African sunset. The

distinctive bluestone building that accommodates the brewhouse and Mitchell's Scottish Ale House is a well-known landmark along Dock Road (opposite left). Here patrons can quaff beer under a star-studded sky or experience the warmth of the hearth in the brewery's pub. For the asking, one can actually see the brewhouse in action (above). This is where the wort, or infused malt, is cooked before it is pumped through a hose underneath Dock Road to a fermentation cellar where it is held for between seven and ten days. Thereafter the beer is pumped to the conditioning cellar where it is kept for three to six weeks. Both cellars are situated in an old tunnel (opposite right) that originally was used to convey stone for the construction of the harbour's first breakwater.

CLOCK TOWER PRECINCT

This statue of a shepherdess and two cherubic figures, at the entrance to the corporate head office of the Board of Executors on Clock Tower Square (left), is a replica of a statue that adorns the old Board of Executors building on the corner of Wale and Adderley streets in central Cape Town. Also located near the Clock Tower is the Nelson Mandela Gateway (right), a triple-storey museum that includes various multimedia exhibitions providing an overview of the history of Robben Island as well as a history of resistance to the system of apartheid. The building was opened by former President Nelson Mandela on 1 December 2001.

ROBBEN ISLAND

This beautiful island is a short ferry ride from the V&A Waterfront. Passenger ferries depart regularly from the Nelson Mandela Gateway near the Clock Tower. Robben Island is where Nelson Mandela and many other opponents of apartheid were incarcerated. Today it is a place of commemoration and reflection. The earliest recorded settlement of the island was when the Dutch used it to gather penguin eggs, slate and sea shells for lime-burning. Later, political prisoners from the Dutch East Indies were banished there. The British used the island as a convict settlement and to establish a leper colony and a lunatic asylum. During the Second World War it was the site for defensive artillery.

NOBEL SQUARE

The idea of honouring South Africa's four Nobel Peace Prize Laureates through sculpture and creating a place of reflection for citizens of and visitors to the country, was conceived by the Western Cape government in partnership with the V&A Waterfront in 2002. Officially unveiled in December 2005, Nobel Square pays tribute to the role the four men played in attaining peace and democracy in the country. The Laureates are the late Nkosi Albert Luthuli (awarded 1960), Archbishop Emeritus Desmond Tutu (awarded 1984), former State President F.W. de Klerk (awarded 1993) and former President Nelson Mandela (awarded 1993). The slightly larger-than-life bronze sculptures are arranged in the form of a crescent

on the square, with Table Mountain as a backdrop. The sculptures were created by the internationally acclaimed Cape Town artist, Claudette Schreuders. A fifth sculpture, *Peace and Democracy*, acknowledges the contribution of women and children in achieving peace in South Africa. Also cast in bronze, this sculpture is the work of Noria Mabasa from Vuwani in Limpopo province. Mabasa uses Venda myths and legends in her work. The unveiling of Nobel Square was attended by two surviving Laureates and Dr Albertina Luthuli, who represented her late father. The Nobel Square Project enjoys the blessing of the Norwegian Nobel Institute. Nobel Square is situated in the heart of the V&A Waterfront between the Victoria & Alfred Hotel and the old power station building, now housing the Compact Disc Wherehouse, and can be reached from Dock Road.

IKHAYA AFRICAN RESTAURANT

For visitors and locals alike in search of authentic African food, Ikhaya African Restaurant in the Clock Tower Centre is the place to go. Ikhaya is Xhosa for 'home', and at home is exactly how patrons are made to feel as soon as they step through the door. Delectable dishes from southern and central Africa are served with orders of traditional African beer. Chef Nomsa Madlala (bottom left) is responsible for a show-stopping menu that includes items such as Go Wild steak and traditional samp and beans. The service is impeccable and the atmosphere spirited. As night falls, performances by a marimba band and djembe drummers set the tone for an exciting evening out.

ALFRED MALL GALLERY

Situated in the heart of the world-famous V&A Waterfront complex, the Alfred Mall Gallery showcases some of South Africa's finest contemporary artworks. The gallery was established in 1994 and has exhibited the works of a diverse range of exciting and talented artists. Open seven days a week, it offers collectors and art lovers from around the world a wealth of choice, including paintings, mixed media, ceramics and sculpture. (Top left to right: Anthony Walton, *Bo-Kaap*, oil on canvas, 90 x 60 cm; Katherine Ambrose, *Before R.D.P.*, acrylic on canvas, 110 x 80 cm. Bottom left: Yoka Wright, *Pathos*, bronze.)

PAULANER BRÄUHAUS

A genuine German microbrewery, Paulaner Bräuhaus has its roots in the early seventeenth century, when the Paulaner monks at the Neudeck ob der Au cloister in Munich began brewing their own Lenten beer. Paulaner Bräuhaus is situated in the Clock Tower precinct and is believed to be the only one in the Paulaner stable situated in a working harbour and which brews its beer below sea level. Bartenders Sabelo Mkwetyana (left) and Washington Mtimkulu (right) raise a toast to the traditional Bavarian Weissbier, smooth Paulaner Lager and Munich Dark made every three or four days on location by brewmaster Wolfgang Ködel. The shiny copper kettles are also used to make seasonal beers for Salvator and Oktoberfest.

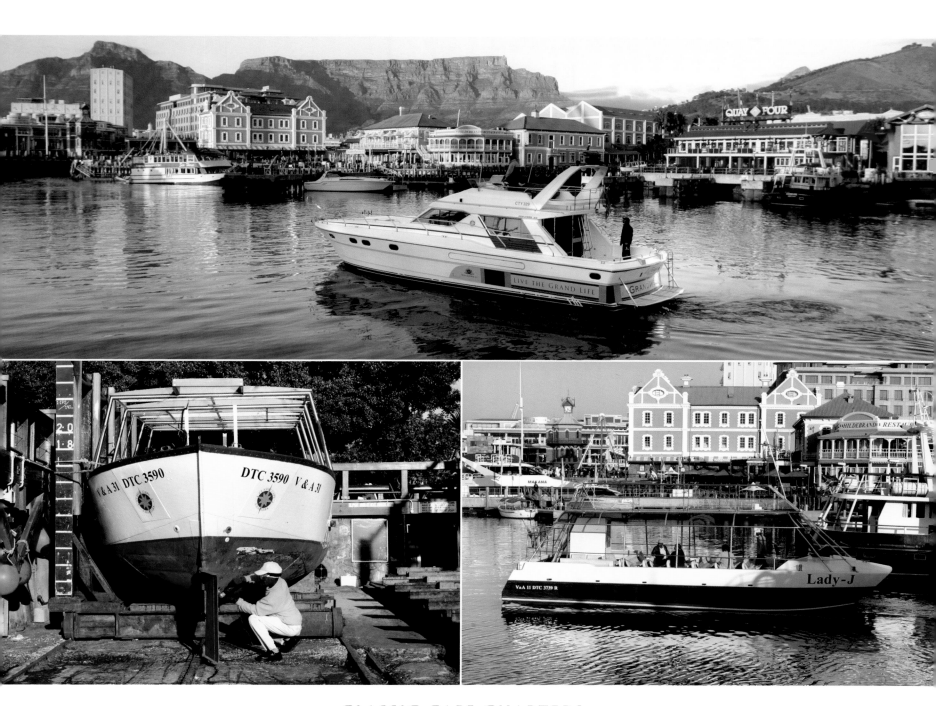

CLASSIC CAPE CHARTERS

Adventure seekers can board Classic Cape Charters's luxurious *La Famiglia* (top) for a cruise along the Atlantic seaboard to Clifton and even to Cape Point via Hout Bay. Fishing enthusiasts can undertake excursions on board the sleek *Wild Thing*. Others can experience the thrills of a working harbour on board the *Lady J* (bottom right) and the *Shosholoza*, which depart hourly from Quay Five and the North Quay respectively. Visitors can also make use of the *Queen Victoria* (bottom left) and the *Prince Alfred*, two water taxis that will ferry passengers to different stops around the V&A Waterfront and its evolving canal system. Whatever your requirements, Classic Cape Charters is bound to have something that will suit your fancy.

BAIA SEAFOOD RESTAURANT

Baia is Portuguese for 'bay' – an apt name that alludes not only to the culinary orientation of this seafood restaurant, but also to its picture-perfect location in the Victoria Wharf along Table Bay. Diners at the wrought-iron tables on the terrace or in the lavish surrounds of the inside dining area are treated to unforgettable views of Table Mountain, a dream setting in which to eat superb food. The menu is an inspired rendition of all things Portuguese. Favourites are Mozambican prawns made with beer, garlic, chilli and cream, and cataplana, a selection of langoustines, mussels, calamari and fresh line fish made in a traditional Portuguese way. Bouillabaisse, prepared in both the French and

Portuguese style, is a speciality. Meat-lovers can choose from a wide variety of dishes including quail, guinea fowl, duck, chicken, beef, lamb and venison. The lunch menu is an adventurous affair, with innovative dishes such as ginger and citrus prawns, octopus salad and salsa of prawn and walnut on the list. The extensive wine list covers the finest the Cape has to offer, including some rare vintages. Owner Luis Viana has paid as much attention to the décor as he has to the food. Tiger-print couches and comfortable chairs are set against prints of works by Modigliani and Henry Moore, creating a sophisticated and intimate ambience.

BUSKING AT THE WATERFRONT

Busking at the V&A Waterfront is of a very high standard and is an important facet of the experience of being there. The word 'busk' – to seek to entertain by singing and dancing – is probably derived from the Spanish word *buscar* or the French word *brusquer*, both of which mean 'to seek'. At the Waterfront a wide range of local musicians and performers are given the chance to strut their stuff, much to the delight of an appreciative audience of local and international visitors. Some enterprising buskers sell 'limited edition' compact discs to music enthusiasts who want to share the experience with family and friends back home. Some of the many street acts found at the Waterfront are the fire-eater

Nwarigha Mutisse (opposite left), the African Dream Marimba Band (opposite right), the Khayelitsha United Mambazo Choir (top right), jazz trumpeter Abe Thomas of the Starlight Band (bottom left), and the Victoria Four (bottom right). The varied sounds and musical styles of these performers add to the vibrant and lively atmosphere of the Waterfront.

FERRYMANS TAVERN

Ferrymans is the oldest of the V&A Waterfront's watering holes. It opened in 1989 as the V&A's first tenant, and it has been going strong ever since. Over the years, Ferrymans has established a firm following of regulars from Cape Town and further afield who flock here to sample its wide selection of beers from around the world and to enjoy the historic atmosphere. The former steam locomotive repair sheds were converted with great skill, and much care was taken to retain the structure and features of the original buildings, including the quarried bluestone walls, distinctive arched windows, Oregon pine beams and teak pillars. The brick-paved floor, stone fireplace and large, old-fashioned bar lend

character to the downstairs tavern. Upstairs, an old world charm pervades the non-smoking restaurant. The atmosphere is enhanced by the exposed stone walls and fascinating photographs of harbour scenes of yesteryear. The restaurant is an excellent place to savour Ferrymans' above average fare, from the traditional fish and chips and curry and rice to specialities such as ostrich or springbok steak. But it is the beers that continue to attract the patrons, so much so that there is standing room only on most weekend nights. In addition to a range of lagers, stouts and ales, the tavern offers its very own Ferrymans Ale – a full-bodied, spicy ale of the traditional Scottish style brewed exclusively for the pub.

A WORKING HARBOUR

When the development of southern Africa's principal freight and passenger harbour into a mixed-use area was first considered, no one could have expected that it would become one of the most successful dockland renewal projects in the world. The original harbour has grown from being a much-needed refuge for ships anchoring in Table Bay into a significant and strategically positioned port on the very busy southern ocean trade routes. The building of the original breakwater began in 1860, when at an official ceremony the 15-year-old Prince Alfred, son of Queen Victoria, tipped the first load of rocks into the bay. The proceedings were attended by the Xhosa chief, Sandile, and the first black

Presbyterian minister, Tiyo Soga. The Alfred Basin was opened ten years later. This was followed by the extension of the breakwater and, in 1905, the building of the Victoria Basin. The advent of larger ships and, later, containerisation necessitated the building of new docks. The Duncan Dock was completed in 1944 and the Cape Town Container Terminal in 1977. Today, the Port of Cape Town operates twenty-four hours a day, seven days a week, and is fully equipped to handle all types of general and containerised cargo. Although the Alfred and Victoria basins are at the heart of the V&A Waterfront, they nevertheless remain an active part of the port, providing facilities for smaller commercial vessels, including fishing and pleasure boats and passenger cruise ships.

HIGH AND DRY

The Robinson Dry Dock was named after the Cape Governor, Sir Hercules Robinson, in 1882. Situated at Victoria Basin, it is used to inspect, maintain and repair the hulls of ships. It takes some three hours to flood the basin of the Robinson Dry Dock, after which the vessel in need of repair is floated into the dock. Once it is aligned with the keel blocks at the bottom of the dock, the entrance gate is moved into position. The water is then pumped out to allow the vessel to come to rest on the blocks. Beams to steady the ship are placed between the sides of the dock and the vessel. The Robinson Dry Dock has a docking length of 161.2 metres, a width at the entrance top of 20.7 metres and a depth of

7.9 metres. Other ship repair facilities at the Cape Town port include a second dry dock, the Sturrock Dry Dock, which has an overall docking capability of 369.6 metres in length and is 14 metres deep, a patent slip to winch ships out of the water for repairs and maintenance, and a synchrolift, capable of handling ships up to 61 metres in length and weighing 1 806 tonnes.

THE TIES THAT BIND

The bollards, winches and rings of the V&A Waterfront have a romance all of their own. For some they are silent witnesses to events of long ago: sailors reaching safety after a tempestuous ocean crossing, soldiers setting off for war, children becoming separated from their parents in a muddle of passengers, and the arrival of the Union-Castle mailship, bringing goods and tidings from afar. For others, they are reminders of important historical events such as the arrival of the American Confederate supply ship, the *Alabama*, in 1863 or the visit by the British royal family in 1947. But then again, they could just be a convenient place for 'sitting on the dock of the bay and watching the tide roll away'.

OF BOLLARDS, WINCHES AND LEANING TOWERS

In earlier days, sailing vessels arriving in Cape Town harbour had to be warped into the Alfred Basin. Warps would be run through sheaves and then tied to windlasses and bollards fastened to the quayside. Some of the yellow-painted bollards seen around the Waterfront today were made from old cannons. All harbour activities would be closely observed by the port captain whose office was in the Victorian Gothic-style clock tower (opposite right). Over the years the building began to lean slightly, and brass supports were used to check future movement.

TIME BALL TOWER AND WEATHER-VANE

Constructed in 1894, this time ball tower (left), now a historical monument, is situated on Portswood Ridge. The first time ball, invented by Robert Wauchope, a Royal Navy captain, was tested in Portsmouth, England in 1829. A time ball is a signalling device whereby a painted ball is dropped at a predetermined time, usually at 1 pm (except in the United States where they were dropped at noon), to enable ships in port to set their chronometers. The ball was raised just before 1 pm and the time was recorded when the ball began its descent. An instrument of a different sort, the weather-vane (right) near the Alfred Mall depicts the V&A Waterfront logo.

70

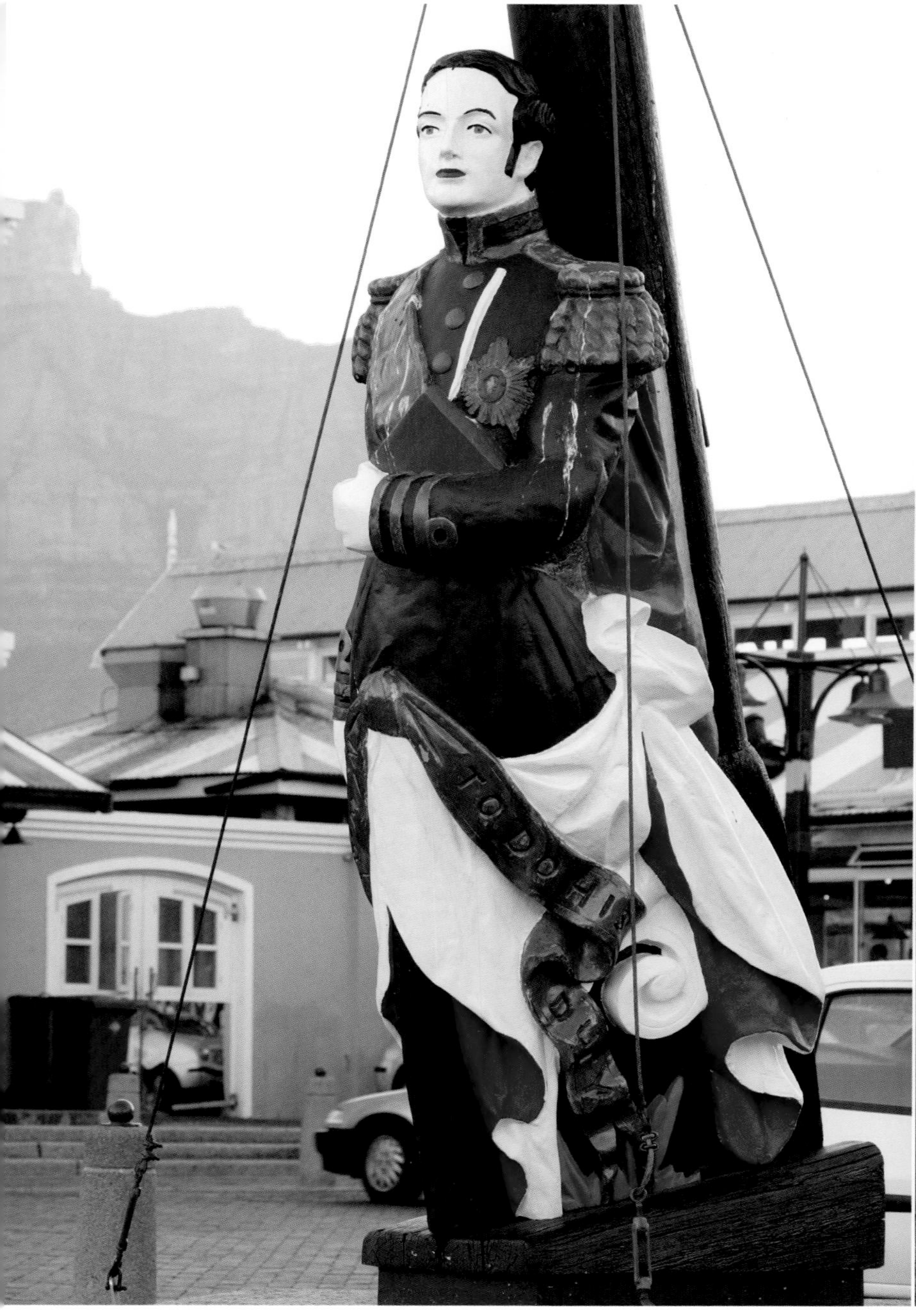

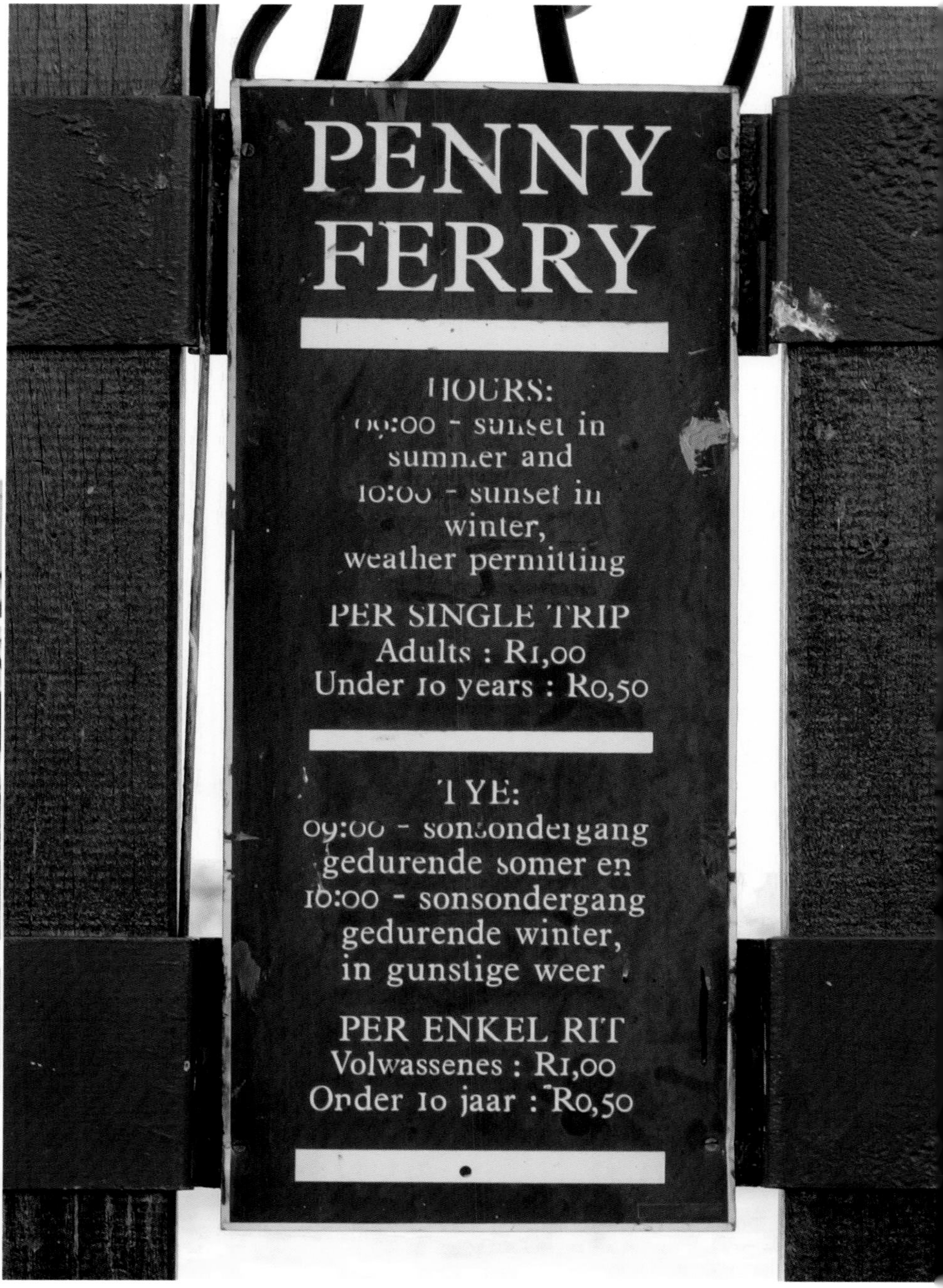
PENNY
FERRY
HOURS:
09:00 - sunset in
summer and
10:00 - sunset in
winter,
weather permitting
PER SINGLE TRIP
Adults : R1,00
Under 10 years : R0,50
TYE:
09:00 - sonsondergang
gedurende somer en
10:00 - sonsondergang
gedurende winter,
in gunstige weer
PER ENKEL RIT
Volwassenes : R1,00
Onder 10 jaar : R0,50

NAUTICAL ADVENTURES

A replica figurehead of the British admiral, Lord Horatio Nelson (left), stands sentinel on the Pierhead at the V&A Waterfront. The original carving washed up on the shore of Bloubergstrand in the early 1900s. The legend on the swag is Nelson's famous order to the fleet at the Battle of Trafalgar: 'England expects every man to do his duty.' Elsewhere on the Pierhead, near this sign (above right), visitors were once rowed across the entrance to the Alfred Basin. A one-way trip on the Penny Ferry took all of four minutes. The Penny Ferry was introduced in 1871 to row harbour staff from one quay across to another. In 1880 the service was opened to the public. The fare? One penny.

A BIRD'S-EYE VIEW

An elegant swing-bridge links the Pierhead, dominated by the landmark old Port Captain's Office building, and the Clock Tower Precinct, named after the historic Clock Tower, a provincial heritage site. The bridge, completed in 1997, crosses the entrance to the Alfred Basin (at left in this photograph). Built of steel and timber, the pedestrian crossing weighs 12.5 tonnes and is 34 metres long. The bridge won its designers, Henry Fagan & Partners, awards from the South African Association of Consulting Engineers and the South African Institute of Steel Construction. The Victoria Wharf Shopping Centre, situated along Quay 5 and Quay 6, can be seen in the background.

SEALS AT PLAY

Cape fur seals (*Arctocephalus pusillus pusillus*) are an integral part of the Waterfront experience, never failing to amuse and delight visitors with their antics as they lie upon old tractor tires fixed to the harbour walls, dive for fish, frolic in the water and bask in the sunshine, occasionally raising a flipper as if to greet passers-by. It is indeed a privilege to see them amidst the hustle and bustle of the Waterfront since seals are generally only to be seen in colonies on rocky offshore islands. These marine mammals have tiny external ear flaps that close over the ear opening when they dive. They use their fore flippers for propelling themselves gracefully through the water and their hind flippers for steering.

THE TABLE BAY HOTEL

Inspired by the commanding panoramic views of mountain and sea, the designers of the five-star Table Bay Hotel have created a landmark in perfect harmony with the natural beauty of its surroundings. Guests can be forgiven for thinking that they have woken up in paradise – all 329 spacious luxury guestrooms and suites look across to Table Bay and Robben Island, or up at the famous Table Mountain. And although the design of its façade borrows from the Victorian architecture of the wharfside warehouses that once populated the old harbour, the interior is dazzlingly modern. Each room is sublimely comfortable, and the bathrooms, facilities and technology are state-of-the-art. For added

convenience, the hotel has its own health spa, gym and heated swimming pool. The grand foyer is framed by enormous glass windows that let in copious amounts of natural light as well as dramatic vistas of the mountain and the adjacent harbour. The harbour-side entrance to the foyer is graced by a giant seal statue. The foyer leads to the lounge, where high tea is accompanied by the tinkling sounds of a baby grand piano. In winter the flames of a crackling log fire dance to its tune. Fine dining can be enjoyed in the hotel's Atlantic Restaurant or the more intimate Conservatory Restaurant. Conveniently located in the heart of the V&A Waterfront, the Table Bay Hotel is also the perfect venue for conferences, business meetings and weddings.

CAPE GRACE

The internationally famous five-star hotel, Cape Grace, is aptly named. Designed by renowned architectural firm, Louis Karol, the four-storey slate-roof building is set on a private quay, a short stroll from the heart of the V&A Waterfront. The hotel is bordered by water on three sides, and overlooks the yacht marina, the Alfred Basin and Table Mountain. The rooms and suites are spacious and feature high ceilings and French doors that open on spectacular waterside and mountain views. At the front is a row of exotic palm trees beyond which elegant yachts and colourful fishing boats lie calm at their moorings.

A DESTINATION OF CHOICE

Cape Grace was conceptualised by hoteliers Charles Brand, his wife Beth and parents Chippy and Cynthia as a rather special establishment that would become the preferred choice for visitors who value personalised service, genuine hospitality and style. It is a tradition continued by its current owner, Meikles Africa. The reception area is one of understated elegance. The hotel's award-winning onewaterfront restaurant has a warm Mediterranean ambience and the excellent food served there is a feast for the eye and palate. Downstairs, the Bascule Whisky Bar and Wine Cellar contains one of the largest collections of fine single-malt and blended whiskies in the world.

JEWEL OF INDIA

A wooden Mogul stands sentinel at an antique door that once hung in a palace in Rajasthan in northern India. Transplanted from its Eastern home to the V&A Waterfront, the intricately carved doorway at the entrance to Jewel of India is a harbinger of things to come. Inside, chefs from India bustle about to produce tantalising tandoori dishes, naan bread, crispy popadums, saffron-coloured basmati rice, tender lamb and curried prawns – dishes to please every palate. The restaurant excels in a style of northwestern Indian cooking called Mughlal, or frontier food, and is rooted in Uzbek, Turkish and northern Indian regional cuisines.

'OLDE WORLD' BARBER SHOP

Enter Mr Cobbs in the V&A Waterfront's Victoria Wharf and it is as if you have stepped into another world. This unique barber shop is reminiscent of the old style barber shops found in Piccadilly, Burlington Arcade or Jermyn Street in Victorian London. 'A cut above the rest', Mr Cobbs offers luxurious hot-towel shaves, haircuts, oriental facial massages and beard trims – all done with the shop's own quality range of shaving soaps, pre- and post-shave balms, shampoos and conditioners. A visit to Mr Cobbs is a must for any man who wishes to take time out to indulge himself in the practice of 'gentleman's grooming'.

THE OLD'E ENGLISH SHAVING SHOP

The Old'e English Shaving Shop is a rather extraordinary specialty shop. This delightful little establishment is crammed with a variety of grooming accoutrements, all painstakingly handcrafted in the same manner they were over a hundred years ago. Shaving brushes are made with resin, nickel silver, English pewter and even Cape silver, and only the softest bristle is used to ensure the ultimate shaving experience. The shaving brushes are all guaranteed to have a lifespan of thirty years! A fine selection of hair brushes, razors, sponges and other toilet requisites such as after-shave lotions and potions are also available. Even a small handmade toothbrush, ideal for the travelling man, can be purchased there.

FLEUR DU CAP

Beautifully displayed bunches of fresh flowers are always on sale at the entrance to Victoria Wharf and elsewhere around the V&A Waterfront. Every September the Waterfront hosts its annual Spring Flower Show to the delight of gardening enthusiasts who visit the show to draw inspiration from the various open-air gardens on Market Square and the Clock Tower Precinct. Leading landscape designers create dazzling displays which introduce both seasoned gardeners and novices to the latest design trends in the use of plants, colour, garden furniture and equipment. The show is also an opportunity to buy plants and garden accessories, become acquainted with new products, and get general gardening advice.

MARION & LINDIE

The Marion & Lindie store in the Victoria Wharf Shopping Centre showcases the very best of this award-winning fashion label, founded in 1994. Today, under the aegis of the House of Busby, it continues to be at the forefront of South African fashion. Lindie Grenfell is the creative force behind Marion & Lindie and creates ready-to-wear designer items of the highest quality, an excellent maternity range, and a handmade couture collection. The store also stocks the Metalicus brand, a stretch-wear basics range created in Australia and the luxury denim brand, 7 For All Mankind. In addition, the store offers an impressive selection of high-fashion accessories.

VAUGHAN JOHNSON'S WINE SHOP

Vaughan Johnson is passionate about South African wine. His eponymous wine shop on the Pierhead at the V&A Waterfront is a venerable landmark. The shop stocks a wide range of the Cape's finest wines as well as epicurean treats such as gourmet cheeses, vinegars and olives. This former winemaker and accountant turned retailer has an encyclopaedic knowledge of the South African wine industry, and is highly regarded as a specialist in the field. A visit to his shop is almost compulsory for tourists and locals alike; if not for enlisting his help in collecting fine wines or getting his opinion on wine prices then at least to purchase that special something to take to dinner tonight.

CHARLES GREIG JEWELLERS

Charles Greig Jewellers is the epitome of elegance and good taste. The dark-green, embossed fabric wallpaper, mahogany furniture and gilt-framed oil paintings of some of the Greig ancestors combine to create an ambience of luxury and privacy. Established in 1899, Charles Greig Jewellers is one of South Africa's oldest jewellery makers. The business has been owned by the same family for six generations. Current owners, Christopher, Donald and Richard Greig manage the activities of six branches in Cape Town, Johannesburg, Sandton and at the Sun City resort outside Johannesburg. The Greig brothers' creativity has been influenced by a succession of artists on the maternal side of the

family. Their grandmother, Elsa Greig, was an artist and also drew cartoons for leading newspapers in the 1940s and 1950s. She was the creative mind behind the image of the Greig stores of that era. Their mother, Italia Greig, is a wildlife sculptor specialising in water birds. Donald Greig (top left) has followed in their footsteps. The business's director and gem and diamond buyer, Donald is also a wildlife sculptor of international renown. In addition to a qualification in gemology from the American Gemological Institute in Santa Monica, California in the United States, he also pursued further training in art and sculpture at the Lorenzo de Medici School of Art in Florence, Italy. His exclusive bronze sculptures can be found in private and corporate collections around the world.

FABIANI

Fabiani has been dressing South Africa's most stylish men since the doors of its first store opened in 1978. Each unique Fabiani outlet carries the luxury Fabiani brand, together with a strong representation of leading designer brands. The distinctive Fabiani collection is typified by its exclusive designs and use of fine fabrics and colour, which reflect an intrinsic quality of happiness. Careful attention is paid to detail – from the overall design of each garment right down to the finishing on each buttonhole. Fabiani caters for the complete men's wardrobe and clients are bound to find something special among its range of formal wear, casual wear, sports wear, denims, shoes and fragrances.

THE FABIANI EXPERIENCE

Fabiani's enormous passion for fine clothes, and its mix of stylish designer menswear, has garnered it a distinguished clientele list that includes many international celebrities, actors, singers, sporting stars, parliamentarians and businessmen. Even women can't resist perusing the elegant collection of the famous clothing emporium. At Fabiani, the shopping experience is always a rich and colourful affair. Expect groovy music, flowers, a glass of the finest malt or even a cappuccino together with well-informed fashion consultants who offer professional advice, thereby ensuring the ultimate customer experience.

SHIMANSKY COLLECTION

On a recent visit to South Africa, Oscar-winner Charlize Theron selected a flawless 47-carat emerald-cut diamond from the Shimansky Collection. Former United States President Bill Clinton thanked the jewellery maker in a personal letter for a gift given during a visit to Cape Town. Both Theron and Clinton are part of a growing coterie of international and local celebrities who admire or wear the exquisite jewellery created in the Shimansky Collection's workshop at the V&A Waterfront. Yair Shimansky, whose fascination with diamonds began almost two decades ago in Japan, is regarded as a leading authority on diamonds, tanzanite, platinum and gold – the signature gemstones and metals of

the Collection that bears his name. Shimansky (opposite) sources all his diamonds from mines in South Africa, ensuring that only conflict-free diamonds sparkle in the rings, bracelets and necklaces created under his watchful eye. These creations include the famous millennium ring designed by Shimansky himself (top left), a collection of fancy yellow diamond rings (top right) and rings set with tanzanite and diamonds (bottom). Visitors to Shimansky's flagship premises at the Clock Tower can pop in at the diamond-cutting works or visit the Shimansky Diamond Museum, which provides an introduction to the science and mining of diamonds.

WATERFRONT CRAFT MARKET & WELLNESS CENTRE

The Waterfront Craft Market & Wellness Centre is home to a creative *mélange* of small business entrepreneurs. Successful stallholders include Selina Dube of Umzamo Curios (top left), whose Ndebele beadwork is in great demand, and artist Salifo Mbombo of Township Arts (bottom right). Jill Neyes works with women from Imizamo Yethu in Hout Bay to produce unique candles and other products that are decorated using painted tea bags (top centre). Wire and recycled objects, often embellished with beads, are perennial favourites (bottom left and centre, top right and centre). A broad range of wellness services and quality products including homeware, furniture, clothing, toys and speciality foods are also available at the centre.

RED SHED CRAFT WORKSHOP

The Red Shed Craft Workshop is a cornucopia of handcrafted items and original artworks. It is where crafters, such as Mary Anne Phillips (top left), can be seen creating the sought-after items for which the V&A Waterfront is famous. Phillips makes appliquéd wall hangings, cushion covers and skirts. Other Red Shed delights include Doris Bruwer's creations made from African fabrics, Zulu beadwork and ostrich feathers (bottom left) and the imaginative 'wearable art' produced by Solveig as an antidote to mass production and uniformity (right).

CANTINA TEQUILA

Mexican cuisine is yet another experience to be enjoyed during a Waterfront visit. Situated on Quay 5, the popular Cantina Tequila has an enviable position, with breathtaking views of Table Mountain, Lion's Head and Table Bay. Its proximity to the departure and arrival point for most harbour cruises means that it is a constant hive of activity as people dash in for a quick bite or relax over a more leisurely meal. The menu offers Mexican classics including national staples such as tortillas, fried beans and nachos. However, no meal is complete without sampling traditional Mexican beverages such as the cantina's own Mexican Chilli Tequila or Corona beer drunk with a slice of lemon straight from the bottle.

PA KUA

Pa Kua is synonymous with stylish contemporary homeware. Exclusive ceramics, exquisite hand-blown glass, and candles imported from France represent just a few examples of the designer home accessories available at Pa Kua. Owner Christiaan Barnard travels far and wide to source the very best designer homeware for his V&A Waterfront shop. An award-winning interior designer, he favours a sophisticated approach that appeals to discerning buyers, especially those with inspiring and creative minds. Pa Kua also stocks a range of exclusive fragrances by some of the world's finest perfumers. Whether you are shopping with a purpose or browsing to indulge your finer self, you are unlikely to leave empty-handed.

BP AFRICA

BP Africa's head office at the V&A Waterfront has been hailed as one of the most innovative buildings in South Africa, and its design is compatible with the petroleum giant's commitment to reduce the impact of its buildings and office activities on the environment. Recessed, double-glazed windows shield the offices from the sun yet let in lots of natural light, resulting in minimal use of the air-conditioning system. Other features include the use of harvested rainwater and recycled water to irrigate the garden and flush toilets, and low-energy lighting and custom-made photovoltaic solar panels to reduce electricity consumption. The panels (top left and right), mounted on the roof, form the largest solar power array in Africa.

DEN ANKER BAR AND RESTAURANT

The distinctive Den Anker on the Pierhead has panoramic views of the working harbour and Table Mountain. Aptly described as 'a corner of Belgium at the tip of Africa', it encompasses the best of both places. Its African Queen Bar is an excellent place to while away the afternoon after a leisurely lunch or to enjoy a pre-dinner drink before indulging in traditional Belgian fare. Menu favourites include succulent mussels served with crisp fries and mustard-infused mayonnaise, melt-in-your-mouth tender pepper steaks, fragrant truffles and North Sea shrimps imported from Belgium. Dessert lovers would not be disappointed with the scrumptious pralines and crêpes flambé on offer. The beer list features some of Belgium's best.

VICTORIA & ALFRED
HOTEL

The luxury Victoria & Alfred Hotel is located in one of the original warehouses built in the historic Cape Town harbour. The North Quay warehouse was constructed in 1904 and was originally used to store coal before serving as a warehouse for the Union Castle Shipping Company and as a customs baggage store. The building was restored in 1990 and converted into the prestigious Victoria & Alfred Hotel. It was named in honour of the Queen of England and her son who visited the Cape in 1870, when Prince Alfred presided over the opening of the harbour. A relaxed and welcoming ambience, coupled with impeccable, friendly and unobtrusive service, will make guests feel right at home. Charming features such as painted ceilings and a wooden staircase add to the romance and intimacy of this privately owned hotel. All of its 94 elegant and spacious bedrooms look out on either the Alfred Basin, Table Mountain or the piazza. The hotel's OYO Restaurant & Cocktail Bar takes full advantage of its location in the heart of the Waterfront, and is the perfect venue for indulging in quayside cocktails at sunset, with unsurpassed views of the working harbour towards Table Mountain. OYO specialises in seafood, which makes it an ideal place for long leisurely lunches of Cape rock lobster, prawns and langoustines accompanied by chilled white wine from the Cape winelands.

V&A MARINA RESIDENTIAL

Set against the dramatic backdrop of Table Mountain and offering spectacular views of Cape Town harbour, Table Bay and the central business district, the luxury apartments and penthouses located in the V&A Waterfront Marina along the Roggebaai Canal represent the ultimate in Waterfront living. Units range from one-bedroom apartments of around 90 m² to luxury penthouses of around 600 m². When complete, the V&A Waterfront Marina Residential will consist of more than 600 luxury apartments and penthouses, with 200 private berths. The prestige of the development is enhanced by the exclusive Cape Grace hotel and South Africa's first six-star hotel, the One & Only, currently under construction.

WATERFRONT BOAT COMPANY

Some of the best sightseeing in Cape Town can be had by water. Sailing enthusiasts can take daily scheduled trips – sunset, champagne or bay cruises – aboard the Waterfront Boat Company's *Esperance* (top left), a Marconi-rigged schooner. The company also runs the *Spirit of Victoria* (top right), with its distinctive red-brown sails and Jolly Roger; the Sea *Princess* (middle left), a luxury foil-assisted catamaran available for charters; the *Jet Boat*, (bottom left, centre and right), which takes visitors to a seal colony; the *Condor*, a favourite with whale watchers; and the *Southern Cross*. Whichever option you choose, you will be treated to unforgettable scenic beauty and thrilling encounters with the Cape's marine life.

HILDEBRAND RESTAURANT

The building now occupied by the Hildebrand Restaurant dates back to 1902 and was the location of Cape Town's first post office before becoming an officers' mess and later the venue for the Harbour Café – a popular Cape Town landmark in the days before the proliferation of restaurants. Today it is occupied by another famous eatery equally renowned for its superb cuisine – especially its seafood platters and authentic regional Italian dishes – and a wide selection of wines from the best of the Cape's vineyards. Owners Aldo and Linda Girolo are familiar faces in this family-run Pierhead restaurant, which, combined with excellent service and a spectacular view, makes dining there an unforgettable experience.

ALBA LOUNGE

Alba Lounge above the Hildebrand Restaurant comes alive after five when trendsetters, lovers, romantics and friends can be found on the outside deck sipping exotic cocktails and watching the tranquillity of twilight give way to the razzle-dazzle of another night at the V&A Waterfront. Inside, patrons can lounge around in style on soft sofas and in plush armchairs – with the added bonus of a crackling fire in winter – or sit at the well-stocked bar or take a seat at the large windows to marvel at the sights and the sounds of a working harbour.

CITY LODGE

The tranquil waters reflecting the City Lodge and the wooden jetty alongside it represent the first stretch of the V&A Waterfront Canal, which flows from the Coen Steytler entrance to the V&A Waterfront to the residential apartment buildings that front the yacht marina. The canal uses fresh water which is regularly circulated through a biological filter. This water will be replaced by seawater in due course. The City Lodge was the first building to be developed at the entrance to the Waterfront. It was a bold and visionary step by hotelier Hans Enderle, whose establishment provides easy access to the Waterfront and is within walking distance of the Cape Town International Convention Centre and central Cape Town.

MAHARANI

Imagine seeing dolphins, Cape fur seals, African penguins, southern right whales, sharks and seabirds. Marvel at Table Mountain, Devil's Peak, Lion's Head and Signal Hill viewed from Table Bay or Robben Island. Sail past the majestic Twelve Apostles towering above the world-famous white sandy beaches of Clifton and Camps Bay and then stop over at Hout Bay. All this can be done from the comfort of the Maharani (Indian Queen), a classic 66-foot ketch that accommodates up to twelve people per cruise. Available daily, the cruises depart from the North Quay of the Alfred Basin in the V&A Waterfront and usually take two hours. Private full-day and overnight charters are also available.

THE PAVILION CONFERENCE CENTRE

Located on the corner of Portswood and Beach roads in the V&A Waterfront, the BMW Pavilion Conference Centre was designed to make the most of its natural surroundings. Built against the backdrop of Table Mountain, it has commanding views of Table Bay and the Waterfront from almost every window in the complex. This setting certainly contributes to its success as a venue for events ranging from business conferences, product launches and corporate functions to cocktail parties, art exhibitions and even weddings. A range of venues to suit a variety of needs and client configurations is available. These span the spectrum from large rooms with foyer areas for display purposes to

smaller, intimate rooms that can be hired for board meetings and the like. All of these come with the latest in audio-visual technology. Further value is added by tailoring additional services such as cuisine, lighting and décor to specific needs. The large exhibition area on the ground floor is also popular for its display of the latest in BMW's range of motor vehicles and motor bikes (opposite top and bottom left). Also located in the centre is the Theatre @ The Pavilion, an atmospheric venue for musical and dramatic performances by South African talents such as Robin Auld (opposite bottom right).

SELECT BIBLIOGRAPHY

Basquart, J. 2000. *The Tribal Art of Africa*. London: Thames & Hudson.

Birkby, R. 1998. *The Making of Cape Town's Victoria & Alfred Waterfront*. Cape Town: V&A Waterfront.

Newall, P. 1993. *Cape Town Harbour – 1652 to the Present*. Cape Town: Portnet.

Worden, N., Van Heyningen, E. and Bickford-Smith, V. 1998. *Cape Town: The Making of a City*. Cape Town: David Philip.

Cape Heritage Trust. 1994. *Cape Town Historical Walk – Waterfront*. Cape Town: Cape Heritage Trust.

INDEX

A page number in **bold** indicates that the reference includes an illustration.

ERRATA

1   The Hoberman Collection would like to
    thank Michael Carney, as well as Tina Alves
    and Lorraine Bester, for their assistance in
    the course of producing this book.
2   Visitors to the V&A Waterfront are serviced
    by retail nodes, the Victoria Wharf
    Shopping Centre, the Clock Tower Centre,
    the Alfred Mall, the Pierhead, and the
    Waterfront Craft Market (p. 12).
3   The annual V&A Waterfront Spring Flower
    Show has evolved into an all-encompassing
    annual floral art competition (p. 81).